Small Press Publishing

The Dos and Don'ts

GW00580142

First published 2020 by Fly on the Wall Poetry Press

Published in the UK by
Fly on the Wall Poetry Press
56 High Lea Rd
New Mills
Derbyshire
SK22 3DP

www.flyonthewallpoetry.co.uk

ISBN: 978-1-913211-07-3

A CIP Catalogue record for this book is available from the British Library.

Contents

Introduction

There is nothing more rewarding than starting your own business – turning your hobby into a full-time career is the dream of many, but very few achieve it. If you feel passionately that you can fill a niche in the publishing industry, but you haven't managed to get your lucky break so far, this book is for you. If you have already started running your own online magazine, small press or are publishing your own work in book form professionally, this book is for you.

There is a lot more to succeeding as a publisher, and as a business, than a good idea. You need to maximise your chances of success. I will take you through the process of branding, working with authors, the publishing schedule, marketing and distributing but first, I'd like to tell you how I started my business.

I run Fly on the Wall Press, specialising in socially conscious anthologies and poetry chapbooks, as well as publishing short story collections. I started the business as a hobby in 2017, publishing my first collection of poetry via self-publishing, under the brand Fly on the Wall Poetry. I learned a lot in the process: editing, proofreading, how to ensure a quality product, and how to reach an international audience through marketing strategies.

The experience was positive, and using social media, I began to develop a supportive network of fellow authors. However, I knew this was a very small operation and I was just one unknown writer in a sea of people submitting their work to magazines and publishers. In order to develop, it was clear that I needed to draw on the experience and the networks of writers before me.

This was when I developed the idea for my first anthology: Please Hear What I'm Not Saying, the profits of which go to

UK charity, Mind. In addition to my own work, I also wanted to publish the work of other writers who were significantly more established than I was.

I thought about the reasons why writers might want to submit their work to me, and what they would feel passionate about as a cause. I knew that mental health affects 1 in 4 people in the UK alone and that the charity, Mind, had a vast amount of support behind it, so when I posted the submission call out on the Fly on the Wall Poetry blog and shared this callout on established poetry networks across social media, I received 600 international submissions.

Suddenly, I had accepted 116 writers who all viewed me as their publisher. I had a lot to learn and I was very lucky to have a friend skilled in graphic design, who worked on both the interior and the cover design for free! Suddenly, I had published a successful anthology, which came runner-up at the prestigious Saboteur Awards 2018 for best anthology, just three months after its release.

It then became clear that I had an online audience waiting for my next submission call and that I had become known as a publisher. Dazed but happy, I decided it was time to make it official: Fly on the Wall Press was born.

Setting goals

After publishing two charity anthologies, I decided it was time to make a profit from the business.

I found myself without a job in September 2018 and signed up to an online mentorship scheme as part of the Prince's Trust, which supports 11 to 30-year-olds who are currently unemployed. Although my mentor did not know anything about publishing, he knew a lot about starting a business and how to market it.

With my mentor's support, I set myself some goals for the business. I developed the tagline: *"A publisher with a difference"*, which later developed into: *"A publisher with a conscience"*, and when expanded: *"Publishing high quality anthologies on pressing issues, chapbooks and poetry products, from exceptional poets around the globe."* I had set myself a niche and an aim – to be the established press for charitable anthologies, and to be known as a quality publisher, evidenced by availability in the UK's most successful bookshop chains and online.

As a publisher, you need a very clear idea about what your books represent and why your publishing niche is important in the industry.

> *First, try answering these questions:*
>
> *Why do you want to open your own publishing press?*
>
> *What previous work experience will help you to do this?*
>
> *What qualifications or training do you have, which will help you with your business endeavour?*
>
> *Which future training courses do you want to complete in order to develop your business?*

Especially on a small press level, you are your own best advocate and if people are interested in your books, it is usually because they are interested in you and what you stand for. To begin selling books, you must be able to sell yourself as a business owner.

Answering these questions will be extremely helpful if you are applying for a grant, or applying for a business loan. Next, you need to decide the basic product you are going to sell. Can you describe what the book will be? Genre, cover design aesthetic?

Once you know what your first book will look like, you need to decide your target audience. Who is your typical customer? For example, I identified that running a publishing press as a young female publisher, my typical customer is roughly aged 25 to 34 years old, and is interested in the arts in general. My audience is predominantly female, middle-class and based all over the world but predominantly, my books are sold in England and the US.

> *So, now that you have developed a customer profile, you can drill down further:*
>
> *How much disposable income does your typical customer have?*
> *When do they spend it?*
> *What jobs do they have?*

What we really want to know now, is what prompts that customer to buy your book or product. For me, I see a peak in sales during the first week of a new book launch. This may be down to the appeal of a new product, but I also attribute this to the strength of the topic covered in the book. For example, if the buyer feels strongly about mental health. Once the book is classed as "old", in my experience, sales will predominantly occur as a result of positive book reviews.

Now you need to decide which factors set you apart, when your audience is deciding who to buy from. The small press market is competitive, and even setting yourself a niche to make your business stand out, will not be enough without a powerful marketing strategy and a quality product.

What is it about your book or your publishing strategy that encourages customers to choose you?

For example, I believe that for Fly on the Wall Press, it's the quality of the books and the diverse range of voices, which we represent.

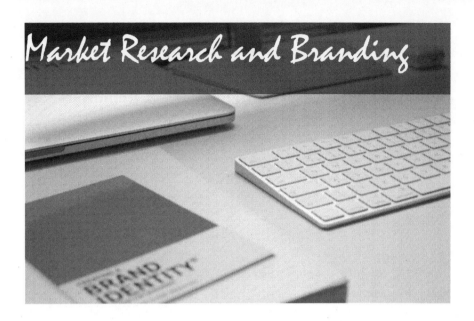

Market Research and Branding

Your hard work in building a brand is taking shape. Before you make any decisions about books and your publishing schedule, you should make sure you have done your research into the publishing market – is your idea viable?

> *For example, if you publish an anthology, and charge £20 for a 200-page book in order to maximise profit, in a market where anthologies in that genre are priced between £8.99-£14.99, you would be doing yourself a disservice and it would be clear that your research into the anthology markets and their current pricing strategies, had been slim.*

Once you have your book idea, you will need to do some field research. This can be as simple as asking friends and family, as well as people working in the publishing industry, about your business/book idea and whether they would buy it. Make sure to get feedback on design aesthetics, as this is why people will pick up your book in-store or online.

For example, it is important to get feedback on your logo. I'm no designer – I picked it up as I went along, and I was very grateful to my first book designer who developed my basic JPEG logo into a professional, clean logo, transferable for future book covers, business cards etc. Your logo is the cornerstone of your business and branding, so it is essential that you get it right in the first place, even if this requires some outsourcing/investment (see Finances section).

Once initial ideas are decided upon, ask the opinion of friends and family - does the design look professional? How does it compare to the logos of large publishing houses? Finally, make sure you have done your research into the various different printers available - customers will appreciate the quality of paper and binding you opt for. You need to find the right balance between quality and price.

A whistle- stop tour through binding and paper quality

Book Cover Options

Paperback - Full-colour laminated cover with perfect-bound binding.

Hardcover - Available with or without dust jacket.

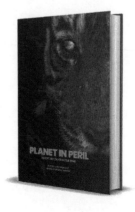

Book Textures

Matte - Soft feel, no glare, polished.

Gloss - High shine, smooth finish.

Book Binding

Perfect Bound - Pages and paperback cover glued together at spine.

Saddle Stitch - Pages and paperback cover stapled together along spine, one inside the other (usually 48 pages max).

Case Laminate - Pages glued to hardcover at ends.

Paper Weights

74 gsm – Standard Trade thickness. Very much 'without thrills' in quality.

104 gsm – 'Quality' thickness. Great for line drawings/ illustration.

115-130 gsm – Great for magazines and photography.

Which is the right paper for my book?

Offset papers are a good all-round economic paper with a reasonable bulk for a quality feel.

A popular choice for academic and business books.

Bookwove papers are a bulkier paper designed to give books a high-quality feel. Not suited to heavily illustrated work.

A popular choice for novels and poetry books.

Silk papers are designed to give excellent quality reproduction but the coating means reduced bulk.

A popular choice for highly illustrated books. (I use this for my magazines.)

During this initial research, you have started to contextualise your publishing endeavour within the wider publishing market and you've started to think about the quality and presentation of your work. A quick way of realising the strengths and weaknesses of your publishing press is to conduct a *SWOT analysis* and then decide on your unique selling point.

Strengths
Weaknesses
Opportunities
Threats

For example, this is what I originally wrote for Fly on the Wall Press:

Strengths: *High quality writing – not afraid to make a statement*

Weaknesses: *I'm a one-woman band and can't do all the projects I wish I could do*

Opportunities: *Poetry and education – working with schools*

Threats: *Poetry is a niche market*

Unique selling point: *Poetry that makes a difference - my books all have a socially conscious element*

Now it's your turn to think about your own SWOT analysis!

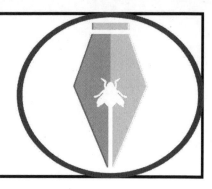

Branding

Branding for your business

The easiest way to progress your press is to have consistent branding. This does overlap with your business plan and marketing strategy because it requires some forward planning!

Your tagline - how can you summarise your business in one sentence which can be easily remembered and repeated by your customers?

Examples:

Fly on the Wall Press: A publisher with a conscience
The Emma Press: Small press, big dreams
Verve Poetry Press: A brand-new poetry press for Birmingham

You may feel overwhelmed summarising your whole press into one tag line. (You may conclude the aims of your press are too broad.) An alternative would be to write a mission statement which you can place on your website and perhaps in your books. This would explain what your press sets out to do, what you stand for, why it was founded in the first place and where you want to go in future.

Branding for your books

Design

Take it from me, planning the design aesthetic for a season of books is a very useful tool for branding. Consistency of text placement on the cover, positioning the author's name on the front and spine, deciding where to place the logo, and what font you choose, are all important.

What colours will dominate your first season? Verve Poetry Press do this very well. Pink, yellow and black, feature on a white backdrop on all their books. While each design reflects the individual themes of that book, the consistent colouring, logo and title placements, enable the reader to immediately identify these books with the publisher.

Cover design is a delicate art – your best bet (and cheapest option) is to send several alternatives to friends and family, to see which they think is the most eye-catching. This is very effective for me as none of my circle read poetry, so the cover must be extra special to get them to pick it off the shelf! Eye-catching doesn't necessarily mean colour – stripped back minimalism can be just as powerful but, in the end, design is a subjective art.

Book interior design is just as important. I've seen many small publishers misjudge their margins, resulting in text "falling into" the spine. The best way to avoid this is to get a physical proof or ask your chosen printer how tight the binding is, so that you can ensure the correct clearance in millimetres or centimetres from the edge of the page.

Look at the books on your shelf: what seems to be the standard font size and style? What is the size, font and position of the page markers?

The art of interior design is subtle, but immediately clear when done wrong.

Online Presence

Once you have established your niche and a tagline for your business, it should be easy to fill out social media profiles for your publishing press. Keep these as consistent as possible - tell people what you do and what you stand for.

Social media will require time and effort to generate audience engagement. Twitter especially, has a strong and responsive writing community, and getting this community to respond to your posts doesn't always have to be work-related. In fact, potential customers will appreciate a business with a personal edge.

You will need to link your social media back to your website, but keep it simple. Aim to keep the look consistent with your social media pages, perhaps taking inspiration from the fonts and colours in your logo.

In the beginning, I would recommend only a minimal investment in your website. Perhaps just a landing page with an explanation of what you stand for, what kind of books you plan to publish and a contact form.

If you do not feel comfortable creating a website design yourself, resources such as *fiverr.com* or *peopleperhour.com* have hundreds of designers who would probably knock up a couple of pages for a small fee. This fee can be offset against the hours teaching yourself how to use a design package or website content management system, and the added frustration that might cause.

Once your website is set up, work on building a name for your brand and gaining traffic to your website before you invest further. If the traffic to your website is poor, the money invested in making it look great will be wasted. *(See Finance section for website domain and hosting fees.)*

Finances

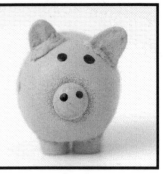

If you want to run a small press, you will be running a business, and your numbers need to be treated as such. It's clear that everyone in publishing is in it for the love of books, but without a commitment to budgets and proper sales accounting, none of our publishing houses would remain in business.

Before you even think about publishing a book or magazine, you need to consider the following:

Website hosting and domain

I don't profess to be a web specialist, so I was happy to utilise web building platforms, such as *Wix.com* or *WordPress.com*, which are based on user-friendly content management systems. I knew I wanted a personal domain name *(flyonthewallpoetry.co.uk)*, which meant I had to upgrade to a minimal premium plan of around £2.50 per month. I bought the domain name from *GoDaddy* which, at the time, was the cheapest option for me. You will find that your first year will be very affordable (99p to £1.99) but be aware that the auto renew will average around £12 per year. You'll find that these initial yearly costs are reasonable, although if you wish to remove advertising pop-ups or add more professional features such as an extensive online shop, inbuilt logo etc., you will increase your costs by £5 to £15 monthly. I would advise saving these additional costs into your second business year – no one expects you to operate on a professional publishing house budget in your first year!

It is worth saying, that the alternative to paying for a hosting website with a content management system, is to pay a designer to create your website from scratch. Both options have their pros and cons, so do your research to work out which option is best for you.

ISBNs

The official Nielsen database *(nielsenbook.co.uk)*, is your go-to resource if you want to be respected as a professional publisher. First, you should aim to list your titles on their database, which is free, six months in advance of publication. You will need to create a profile account on Nielsen's Title Editor for this. The database ensures your titles are visible to booksellers, libraries and other outlets, in over 100 countries. Nielsen is the ISBN agency for the UK and Ireland.

Unfortunately an internationally recognised ISBN costs £89 (£164 for 10/£369 for 100/£949 for 1000), so not the friendliest numbers for a start-up company. However, a Nielsen ISBN will help you to physically get your book into bookshop chains.

Marketing budget

Although this is not the chapter on marketing, it is worth saying that you should allocate a marketing budget per book. This can be as small or large as you see fit, but spend it wisely. Think about what you are prepared to spend on the following:

1. *Review copies* (posting out to the literary magazines, influential book bloggers and journalists)

2. *Social media* (Facebook, Twitter and Instagram are all examples of platforms where you can add a budget to your posts to expand your reach but you should target this form of advertising at users with relevant interests, to avoid wasting this investment)

3. *Google advertising* "Just Google it". You can be sure thousands of people will see your advertisement, but how competitive are you willing to be with your daily budget against other advertisers? Google advertising offers a number of ways to appear on the search engine. This could be through text advertising, whereby you select search engine phrases or words you would like your advert to appear on, or through images which appear on pages relevant to your business. You will be able to set the budget yourself, and Google will suggest how to increase the visibility of your advert by adding budget or new search terms as you go along.)

Smart pricing

You will become best friends with your printer, once you've found the one who will give you the best value for your money, of course. Make sure you get at least 10 quotes for your first book – I'm not kidding. Margin is everything.

I publish primarily poetry and I have established a solid baseline: regardless of size, 36-90 page book (perfect bound, 250gsm, 100gsm interior) will cost me between £1.40 and £1.90. I give my authors 40% net profit, so the process divides like this:

Book: (40 pages) RRP £6.99

Cost to print: £1.60

Net profit to author: £2.16

Net profit to publisher: £3.23

£3 profit per book should be your baseline, more where you can get away with it! Poetry as an industry isn't particularly well valued in terms of the number of people who want to pay for it. £6.99 offers both a good profit margin, and a smart price based on similar poetry collections of this size. If you scale this up and we imagine you sell 200 copies with the £3.23 profit margin, you'll have £646 per title.

If you work yourself to the bone and publish 24 books in your first year, you're looking at an annual salary of £15,504. (No one ever said publishing would make you rich, but you certainly won't ever be bored.)

The profit and loss sheet

Learn to love your spreadsheet. I do! It's my bible and my brain. A year ago I hated accounting, but those spreadsheet cells and formulas will grow on you. When I took my business full-time in September 2018, I found myself an online mentor via the Prince's trust, Will Lock, who first gave me my now invaluable profit and loss Excel sheet.

I account my book sales like this:

1. Direct sales

2. Ingram (external distribution) sales

3. Amazon e-book sales (if separate)

4. Costs (marketing/setup fees/stock/venue hire/postage)

They look something like this:

Direct sales - July 2019

Quantity: 1

RRP:£6.99

Cost:£1.40

Gross profit:£6.99 - £1.40 = £5.59

Net profit:£6.99 - £1.40 - website sale fees - postage

Author net profit: £6.99 - £1.40 x 40% (- website - postage fees)

My monthly profit is cumulative, so I can track each title's individual profit and have a business total of all the books sold so far, on a separate Excel tab. I also indicate when Ingram/Amazon sales will be paid – typically 90 days after sale. This does mean your cash flow is often vulnerable, so make sure you account for this.

"Easy" Money

It is your legal obligation to send your books to the British Library one month after publication under the *Public Lending Right scheme (PLR)*.

You may also receive a request to send your books to a further five libraries across the UK, but this only becomes a legal obligation if you receive this correspondence. The cost of book printing and postage to the PLR scheme can seem like an unfair expense for the publisher. The good news is you can register to receive money from PLR each time one of your books is borrowed from the library under the scheme (you can check online which countries are registered).

As an editor, your legal right is 20% but if you feel your contribution was more substantial, you may register for 50% (they may ask for evidence of this). You are required to register your titles before June 30 each year and any profit will be paid the following January.

Another scheme which will provide you with this kind of passive income, is the *Author Licence Collecting Society (ALCS)*. It is free to join and simple to use. Using the ISBN, you can list your contribution to each title: book, script or article. The agency tracks how many times each title is photocopied and pays its members twice a year. Your first payment will be an accumulation of years of licensing fees which you may not even be aware you are owed. The agency takes roughly 8% of each payment, but as this is money you wouldn't have access to without the agency, it seems like a reasonable fee.

My first payment was £180.

Book design

As this is the Finance chapter, we are not going to talk about the aesthetics here, but the different routes to book design.

1. The do-it-yourself route

Book design may seem impossible and impenetrable to learn, if you are not familiar with design software. If you are not computer-savvy, it is worth saying that this route may not be for you and the initial investment of a book designer, could be a much more straight-forward route for you. However, after a few weeks of pulling my hair out, I found it easy to teach myself. The easier software to use is Adobe InDesign (for interiors and covers) or Adobe Photoshop (cover design and photo editing). These packages and subscriptions are available to purchase separately or together.

2. *The designer*

The artwork, cover layouts and interior typesetting and layout: three expenses you will end up paying freelancers to do should you choose not to purchase design software. Freelancers all work to different rates but you will find fair pay rates for design work, on the Society of Authors page to guide you. There are many places to find book designers online, so make sure you do your research and compare both the quality of their work and portfolio against the quotes.

Legalities

Any good publisher should have a watertight, legally registered company, either as a sole trader or a limited company. You will also need business insurance to protect you from any contract or legal disputes; for example, if you are not paid for a shipment of books. You should do your research on this – the website *simplybusiness.co.uk* is a good place to start, and using a broker to find me a suitable insurance deal, made my process a lot easier. Any book publishing contract should be written in legal language and outline the terms of agreement between you and your author. Your promises will cover:

Royalties - the percentage net profit your author is entitled to from each format, and any advance payment.

The production - From accepting the work, what timeline do you agree to work to?

Your rights as a publisher - i.e. the final say on any design; any formats you wish to have a monopoly over, which could be e-book, audio and print.

Your author's copyright - which remains with them in all ethical contracts.

You should make sure that your contract covers all eventualities. For example, if an author decides to pull their book halfway through the publishing process, you should be able to refer them to a get out clause. This will cover your costs so far. For example, if you know that your design and admin cost you X amount of hours, and you have an ideal hourly rate of £X, this is likely to be the get out clause paid by the author, should they request to cancel the terms of the contract once signed.

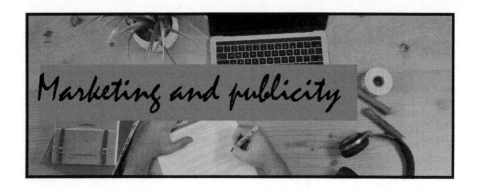

Marketing and publicity

Many would argue that marketing is not the role of the publisher. But no matter how good your books are, or how high the quality of the work, if no one has heard of your brand, your press will fail. Even when outsourcing or delegating areas of my marketing, I still micro-manage, not only because I am incredibly precious about my branding, but because marketing is a genuinely fun and creative process. A marketing plan for a book may look something like this:

- *Press release (copywriting and distribution)*

- *Interview and review coverage*

- *Social media campaign*

- *Events (Book fairs and signings?)*

- *Book launches*

- *Stocking/Contact with Bookshops*

- *Leaflets/Merchandise*

- *Email campaigns*

- *Blog Tours*

Let's look in detail at what each bullet point involves.

The Press Release

Typically, a book launch won't be treated as "news", but more likely a "feature", based on its topic, theme or the geographical location of your author. However, if you can convince newspaper editors that a feature on your book is both relevant and engaging for their audience, you have bagged yourself a campaign to a wide readership and audience you may not otherwise have access to.

Writing the press release

Who? What? When? Why? How? Address these in the first sentence of the first paragraph, if you can. Change the title of the piece to make it specific for the newspaper you are sending it to. Is it of local interest? What part of the book is intrinsically valuable?

In the second paragraph, focus on the gravitas of the author: what story do you want to tell the reader about your author and can you list any big-name influences of the work which the general public will be able to identify alongside your author's work? A quote from your author will add authenticity and character to the piece. A call to action: you must refer readers to your website to read the book – without this detail, the exercise has been wasted.

Distribution

Each newspaper website has a *Contact Us* page, which will usually list journalists names and job titles. Email the most relevant journalist and ensure that your 'Subject' header is attention-grabbing and self-explanatory. For example, *Arts Press Release: Pilot launches mental health memoir"*.

You will need to send a high resolution image of the book cover and preferably the author (300dpi or above).

Then set up a Google alert on your author's name – this is a free service which will flag up any coverage or mentions of your book that you may otherwise have remained unaware of.

Print media is a declining business so think creatively – people read their news online, so online-only newspapers and arts-based websites are a good bet and should not be underestimated. Having said that, different outlets require slightly different tones. Sometimes you can gauge this from recent articles they have published (check the topics they cover, the style used – formal or conversational – the political leaning etc.) Sometimes the focus is on physical qualities or layout – classic or contemporary? You can also make educated judgements based on the following:

Glossy magazines:

Quarterly/bimonthly/monthly

Heavily reliant on paid advertorial. Generally distributed to businesses or supermarkets.

Send your press release two months in advance. Bear in mind the aesthetic: it needs to be high quality and generally aimed at an affluent, older audience. Think regional "life" magazines.

Freebies/roundup:

Monthly magazines - local business based.

Likely to support arts organisations but you need to be able to prove your location is within the audience catchment area. Community angle – this audience is family-based, looking for a 'feel good' story or inspirational events to take the kids to.

Send press release two months in advance.

<u>*Weekly newspapers:*</u>

Regional or national newspapers.

Send press release one month in advance. National coverage is much harder to secure, so to improve your chances, your press release must have national appeal.

Interview and review coverage

Just 10 years ago, the focus of this section may have simply been on how to convince the review section of *The Guardian, The Times* or *The Independent* to feature your books, but times are changing.

I strongly believe in the effect of micro-influencers, by which I mean extremely dedicated followers of your brand and ethos. These influencers believe in your books so strongly that their voices, both off-line and online, can influence the buying patterns of other readers. Suddenly, the common man's opinion becomes important to harness.

There is a large network of book bloggers on the internet and this is becoming an important network of micro-influencers with whom small presses need to engage (your local book club has the same effect). Sending your books to book bloggers ensures impartial reviews that will be read and shared internationally. Equally, most bloggers will be happy to feature your book via a guest post (you may like to ask your author to write a blog post in the process of writing the book) or an interview, which they may conduct themselves or may accept syndicated.

As well as this blogging community, you will need to target literary journals, which often have a dedicated reviewer attached to their publication. Small presses support each other, so think about reviews and interviews accepted by other publishers as a two-way street – *what can you do to reciprocate and how can you share your marketing efforts by working with them?*

Social Media Campaigns

Social media marketing should be fun, however many people tell me they don't have the time, or that they find it hard to gain a following. The fact is, social media has become essential for branding – whether it's the President of the United States or a local author, the reason people choose to follow or engage with you online is much the same:

1. *They want to know who you are in 'real life'.*

2. *They are interested in the content you produce and the conversations you start.*

3. *They attribute a certain level of importance to you.*

As a fledgling publisher, you need a quick way to find an audience, and social media is absolutely fantastic, but you need to make the time.

Any social media campaign for a book should revolve around conversation. You need to produce content such as interviews, reviews, cover reveals, excerpts, graphics, pre-order links and author event promotion. The key to this is the intention – your goal is to get the audience to read your post, but even more importantly, to click on the link through to your review or website. Do not just post a link - social media is full of lifestyle suggestions, so you need to stand out. Whether the reader engages with your post is down to you.

In order to swing conversation your way, or to increase a book's visibility online, you can incentivise. For example, if someone tweets about pre-orders opening, offer them a free chapter to download.

There are already so many books about social media and how to use each platform to your marketing advantage, so I will simply summarise that a social media campaign should have two things: consistency of tone and genuine personality.

Events

As a small press, you may find an effective way to raise your profile and sell books, is to attend (and purchase stalls at) book fairs and publishing/creative writing fairs. You will find this is a great way of networking with other publishers and authors. It is worth approaching these events with a knowledge of your aims from the event. This is because you will find particular writers attend these events to pitch their book ideas – which is great if you are seeking new authors or are open to unsolicited submissions. If, however, your reason for attending a book fair is purely to sell books, you may need to direct them to your next submission call, or flip the question: *"Have you read any of our books? We are looking for authors who know and appreciate the style of our work"*.

Book launches

When approaching a book launch, first consider the following factors:

1. *Price and location of venue.* City or town? Are there easy connections by public transport? Is parking available? What does the venue provide? (E.g. a microphone and projector are valuable additions.)

2. *Marketing strategy* (Does the venue assist with publicity? What will the author contribute?)

3. *What can I do to make the event stand out?* As standard, people expect a reading followed by signing, so what else can you offer? Interesting launches I have attended, have included Q&A sessions (with either the author or a dedicated host), and guest performers or speakers if appropriate. Perhaps you could even combine it with a workshop.

You don't always have to host a book launch for your author – geographically and financially it can be challenging. Moreover, it isn't always expected – authors will often organise their own launch events. However, they are a great way to ensure your immediate audience buys a copy of the book (the author's family and friends) and they generate an immediate return (in that the profit is collected that same day).

Don't view the event in isolation, however.
Documenting your event with blogs, videos and photos, can also give you an invaluable stream of social media fodder for use when the event is over. This maximises on the marketing potential, by engaging an audience who were unable to attend the event. So, if the launch doesn't attract as many people as you originally hoped, don't despair – it is still a really useful tool to get your publishing name in the public eye and you will make meaningful connections, face-to-face, with those who do attend.

Stocking/Contact with Bookshops

High street bookshops, particularly independent businesses, are happy to support local authors and publishers. However, this process can be difficult for a small press publisher if they are not sure how to approach the negotiation. Below is what I have learned about the process and I hope it will be useful to you!

Your selling pitch to a bookshop may be much like an initial pitch to an agent or publisher. You will need a quick synopsis of the book and a couple of lines about who you are.

The sales details need to include the following:

- How much does your book retail for?
- How much are you selling your book to the bookshop for?
- In the UK, this can be anything from a 30% trade discount to a 55% trade discount, which is calculated from the recommended retail price. Bear in mind that in the UK, the publisher is responsible for paying postage of the books to the bookshop.
- You must outline the terms of any book returns.
- Bookshops will be familiar with: "consignment terms" which means that the bookshop will pay for the stock once it has sold and can return unsold stock when it chooses or "sale or return" where the bookshop pays for the stock according to the payment terms (your trade discount), but has the right to return unsold stock.
- You may also want to include a few sample pages for the bookshop to read.
- Outline why you believe this book has marketing potential in their store – in which section do you believe the book should be displayed? Why do you think the book will sell well? You could outline any publicity or marketing plans that you have which could contribute to the book's success.

- You also need to send a JPEG image of the book cover.

Top Tips

Bookshops prefer an email over a spontaneous author visit in person. You could always email to propose a time for your visit if you prefer a personal approach.

Within your email, a link to your book on Amazon should be avoided. Most high street bookshops will perceive Amazon as having a negative effect on physical bookshops.

Supply: can your book be made available through national wholesalers such as Gardners or Bertrams? (UK). Your printer may be able to help you distribute the book via the wholesalers mentioned. For example, a traditional book printer may be able to hold stock of your books and distribute them to bookshops when orders come in. Ingram Spark/Lightning Source will ship your copies to retailers via a print on demand set up. If the bookshop orders copies of your books direct from yourself, agreeing to set up a trade agreement with yourself directly, don't forget to deliver your books with your unique invoice. This ensures that the book-shop has your contact details for future orders and your bank details for payment!

How does a bookshop decide on which books to stock?

For many, representatives brief booksellers on new books and their marketing potential, on behalf of publishers.

Bookshops then make the decisions based on their typical market and the subject of the book.

Leaflets/merchandise

This is by no means an essential marketing strategy, but 'freebies' can be a great incentive for attracting new customers or as a way of rewarding loyal customers for their orders.

Business cards are a standard requirement. Keep them with you permanently so that you always have them on hand for events or any unexpected networking opportunities! At the very least, a business card should include your logo, business name, mobile number, email, website and any social media links or handles.

Quirkier merchandise can be used as a pre-order incentive – for example broadsides, bookmarks, customised mugs or pens could be a gift for customers who are happy to purchase the book as an early investment.

Email campaigns

An e-shot is a valuable marketing tool and will be sent to subscribers to your mailing list. These subscribers are already invested in your work, and they actively want to know about your latest projects before they go public. In return for their loyalty you can offer exclusive subscriber deals, insight into your publishing process and a friendly, engaging public persona. Packages such as Mailchimp allow you to professionally format and send e-shots to your mailing list – some are free up to so many addresses, and they look after the GDPR legalities, like offering an 'unsubscribe' function. You may also have these inbuilt with your website – within the Wix.com system, there is an option to compose email campaigns.

Blog Tours

You can organise a Blog Tour for your book yourself or employ a Blog Tour organiser (see resource list at back of the book for some known Blog Tour organisers).

Essentially, a Blog Tour is a number of consecutive days in which your book is featured on a number of book bloggers websites, through excerpts, interviews and reviews. There will be a Blog Tour poster showing on which days the book will feature on which blogs, and you will need to provide the book in physical or e-book form for reviewers based on their preference.

Typically, the Blog Tour will take place in the lead up to your publication date to generate excitement.

Case Study

Creating an anthology from start to finish

I want to share with you what I have learnt over the years about creating an anthology and how to work with various different writers within the book to ensure success.

The submission call

Guidelines are the bane of every publisher's life – you will find that many submissions ignore them! Therefore, the aim is to make your submission guidelines both clear and brief. Here is an example of a submission call for the Fly on the Wall Press magazine:

Magazine Guidelines

We are open! The theme is 'Chaos'. We are looking forward to reading your work!
Submissions will close on October 30th.

The webzine will be available to download as an ebook or purchased as a print edition. Contributors will receive a free PDF download and will be paid any royalties generated from the first month's sales.

Submissions will be forever free - but please consider buying a book or ebook from the Fly on the Wall shop as without this the press cannot survive! If you are based outside of the UK, please note that we can only pay royalties via PayPal.

Guidelines:

Please note, for the ebook edition, written pieces requiring strict page form may not be appropriate, for example, shape poetry.

Poetry

Please send up to 3 previously unpublished poems (with exceptions for poetry which has been featured in the past on social media or blogs) on a word doc, one poem per page.

Poems should be no longer than 40 lines.

Please send a short bio of roughly 2 - 3 sentences.

Send to (EMAIL) with the subject line 'Magazine/First Name Last Name'.

You can expect to hear back within 3 - 4 weeks; feel free to get in contact after a month if you have not heard from me.

FAQ

How do your royalties work?

Writers are paid 50% net profit of any sales within the first 30 days of the magazine's release. This is because the magazine will have a Print On Demand set up and paying royalties indefinitely creates a lot of work! Royalties will be paid via bank transfer (UK) or Paypal. If you are not based in the UK, please note that royalties can only be paid via Paypal.

Marketing the submission call

You will be able to find national and regional *submission call roundups*. You can usually find a contact email on these websites or social media forums to ask the host to add your submission call to the list.

Email newsletters - from publishers or writing opportunity forums such as UK companies *New Writing North, South* and *East Midlands* have large readerships and typically have an email at the bottom to send your submission call to.

Social media – information moves fast, so you can get away with mentioning your submission call out frequently throughout the weeks and months.

Word-of-mouth – if you are attending a spoken word event, the hosts usually don't mind mentioning your opportunities!

The Reading

What do you want from the anthology? If the anthology is themed, how can you shortlist submissions based on the topics and viewpoints you want to represent? If the anthology is not themed, have you represented a wide range of stylistic choices, genres and ages?

Accepting submissions

I typically draw up an anthology contract. This allows me to get shipping addresses early, and allows me to have written consent to use the writers' work in the anthology, which avoids any legal problems further along the line, although thankfully, I have never encountered any problems! As my anthologies fundraise for charity, my contract always includes a clause that the author consents to waive any royalties generated for our chosen charities. I also outline that the author is entitled to a free copy of the anthology.

Throughout the years, I have developed various models for this. For my first anthology, working with a budget of £0, I set the price of the anthology to the cost price on Amazon, and contributors bought the book direct from Amazon three days before the official release, when I put the price back up to £10.99, for customer purchasing. For this anthology, contributors did not have to pay to submit and the submission call was open internationally.

For my next anthology, I asked for a submission fee of £2 for an unlimited number of poem submissions. I ordered a print run of hundred books initially, and posted the books out for free internationally to contributors. *This cost me roughly -£200 despite the initial fee to submit and meant that the anthology struggled to make ends meet.*

For my third anthology, (an expensive colour hardback), I set submissions up as a competition, £5 per poem or artwork, with prizes available in each category and a number of sponsored free entries via the kindness of a pay it forward scheme. *Despite this fee, I still found the project suffered from sending the free copies internationally (-£300) and it took a small crowd-funder to get us back on our feet.*

Going forward, I am looking at giving free copies to contributors internationally, but putting a clause in the contract that international contributors will receive a digital copy, and a physical copy should they be happy to cover postage.

The above models are based on the charity aspect of the books. If your books are for profit, you may not find international postage as prohibitive.

Sorting

I then look at dividing the poems into sections based on themes and potentially styles. I then dedicate page proofs with a deadline for the poet or writer to return with their comments over email. If you don't set a deadline for this, you may find yourself endlessly chasing your writers!

Throughout the production process, I like to keep my anthology contributors updated and engaged with:

The cover progression

The marketing material

Any events scheduled

Pre-orders opening

If my contributors are engaged in the project, I find they are the best advocates of the book and their word-of-mouth is a useful marketing tool.

Publicity

1 to 2 months before publication

I source reviews and competitions which may benefit the book and expand its readership.

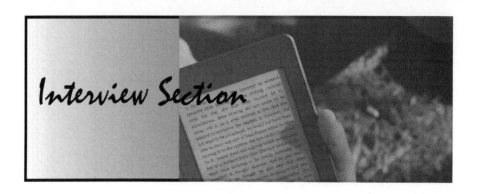

Interview Section

This section draws upon the experience of small press publishers in various genres. I have conducted a series of interviews with the managing directors/founding editors of each publishing press and I hope you will find their process and history as fascinating as I have found them!

HVTN PRESS

In Conversation with Andrew Wells, lead editor for HVTN Books.

Andrew is based just outside of London and works in trade publishing after recently graduating UEA's English Literature with Creative Writing BA. He has reviewed for Glasgow Review of Books and his essay 'Waiting for Goals' is published with Fanzine. His poetry has appeared in Poetry Wales, Elbow Room, The Interpreter's House, 3:AM Magazine, Lighthouse, Bare Fiction, Amberflora, Tentacular, and Sharkpack 2014-2017, among others. His first pamphlet was J/W/U (PYRAMID Editions, 2016). Contact: haverthorn@gmail.com

About HVTN Books.

"We seek writing that resists simple classification and easy escape, writing greater on the inside and than the sum of its parts. HVTN's two series, Books and Interruptions, are curated by Andrew Wells and Iris Colomb respectively. With our new artist-book imprint, Interruptions, we aim to open up a space for projects that don't fit the standard formats. We want to publish experimental books and poetic artefacts whose forms are inexorably tied to their contents and whose contents are tied to their forms, creating opportunities for poets and language artists to take full creative control."

How many people are in your team, either paid or voluntary, and how do you divide your roles?

Two people (myself and co-editor Iris Colomb). I don't draw payment and instead re-invest sales in the press. Iris is paid a small stipend per publication she is directly involved with. She worked on the magazine and is now starting a series called Interruptions for which she'll receive similar payment to the authors. Iris also gives a lot of support for events and on the books I solicit for no pay. We divide our roles by having separate projects, which we each help one another with. It means we can both be autonomous in our worlds; we can be control freaks. But I think things are more relaxed when someone says 'hey, I really think you should (or should not) do this thing', because it's advice out of care that doesn't get confused for a power struggle (which can become the case if you both have to approve submissions).

What genre of books primarily do you publish and how many a year on average?

The magazine was bi-annual but that's on a hiatus now that we're aiming to average about 3-4 poetry collections a year. Once we're in a good rhythm with that, or if we need a break from poetry collections, the magazine may come back. For Interruptions I expect to be publishing 2 or 3 a year, but right now we're in the middle of our first submission call and these things can be hard to predict. For our poetry collections, I'm looking for work in long form, de/re-constructed novels seem to be our thing – that covers Misherit, Strays, Umber and, arguably, Astropolis and Box. Each of those poetry collections is concerned with world-building or breaking. We're also interested in collaborative work, our first title (Strays) was a collaboration between Julia Rose Lewis and James Miller, and our next book (Nemeses) is second selected collaborations of SJ Fowler – the first volume was published by the excellent Penned in the Margins.

When did your press open for business and what was your first year like?

HVTN started in late 2014 as a magazine, publishing poetry and short fiction. Our first year was fun and stressful and we sold a handful of copies. We started as print-on-demand but have since moved away from that model.

What are the most rewarding things about running a small press?

The reading. I really like reading the books I publish; before, during, and after publication. I like getting to collaborate as an editor on work that influences my own poetry and thinking, that's a huge privilege – to know the authors and the work so well, of books that hold a lot of meaning for you. Also bringing people together and connecting writers in some way. I remember attending a reading in London where the organiser (Richard Skinner) had brought one of the readers (Tara Skurtu) over from Romania after being connected through HVTN. They were both in our first issue, so this was quite early on and made the stress as a young editor feel worth it.

What are the most challenging things about running a small press?

At first, money. I paid for the website using my savings from coaching football at 14, then I worked a lot of extra hours, double shifts as a bar-back, barista, shop assistant, to keep the press going during sixth form and university. Now that I've graduated and got a job that pays ok, money is easier. I still want to be self-sustaining as a press but it means we can pay authors, be more generous on author copies, take projects on a little further in advance. That's a load off. I would say the hardest thing now is working with distributors and some bookstores, negotiating returns and discounts is hard when you're doing print runs of 150 copies. Say you've an order of 50, and then it's returned, the chances are you've had to go back to the printers to order 50 more, and now you'll never shift those 50 or make the money back. Any of those 50 you did sell will be at a 30-50% discount too, so very little of the RRP comes back to the publisher.

What do you take into consideration when considering manuscripts and how do you compile your season of publishing (if this is curated in any way?)

It's absolutely curated, I take great pride in having a line-up of books that speak to one another but – also I think – continue to move the conversation on. I think 2020 will see fewer books fitting that novel description and more collections of short poems, but these collections show how that can be done whilst traversing a lot of ground – rather than pandering to the fairly common Faber-esque 40-50 pages of short poems.

They'll be like 3 disc albums, more Brawlers, Bawlers, & Bastards.

Do you advertise manuscript submissions? If not, how do you approach authors or agents? If you do, how do you spread the word and how many manuscripts do you expect to receive in a typical reading period?

Interruptions we've been advertising, it's a new project and a very specific call for work that breaks the traditional format of a book. A handful of presses (I think of Zimzalla, Ugly Duckling, Guillemot) have done similar work. So we're trying to get the word out there. For the existing series of poetry collections, we get enough strong submissions whether we advertise or not. Occasionally, I will approach an author directly if I really like their work. We haven't really dealt with agents, I think we're too small for that, and agents are less common in poetry anyway.

What does a typical book marketing plan look like for you?

We wing it. A lot of planning goes into events, where we sell a few books and they're good publicity because the events are good (good poetry, accessible and welcoming spaces). With the exception of the BOX launch, I should say – that was in a bookshop basement, though we would have used the ground floor if they had let us. We tweet, we send out review copies – that's often a black hole because reviewing is quite a thankless (unpaid) task in poetry. We take punts on the prizes. I have reservations about prize culture. And the setup doesn't favour small presses; if you can nominate 8 books, for example, that benefits a press that can publish 8 books a year. Bigger presses can simply buy more tickets in the raffle. But, I think putting the books forward is only fair to the authors.

How do you continue to build your brand within a busy market?

We have a recognisable house style, both interior and exterior. There's room for play and change within that mould to keep things fresh, but keeping that within a house style gives us an identity.

And on a perhaps shallower note, I really like seeing the spines match up on my own bookshelf. For the Books series, at least, it's in my vision and aesthetic, so part of publishing with HVTN and part of the submission process involves checking that authors buy into that. Otherwise there's conflict down the road. If I know an author hates the house style, I don't take them on. A part of me wonders why one would submit if you don't like the image of the press, but on the other hand, I appreciate submission is a tough, long, gruelling process, and sometimes there aren't loads of places open where you can send for free. So, that part of the selecting is perhaps a harsh reason to say no (especially as that reason will come up after I've said I like the poems), but better than having either author or publisher concede down-the-line and being unhappy with the book after all the work that goes into it, on both sides.

What parts of the publishing process do you do in-house and which do you outsource?

We've outsourced for the house style on our first book (Strays), but adapt it ourselves for new titles. One book for typesetting, that's it. And unless in a pinch with workload, we probably won't do so again – it's too expensive. Between us, Iris and I do the copy editing, any in-depth line editing, typesetting, proofreading, packaging, posting, sorting payments, covers, reading and responding to submissions, updating and designing the website (albeit through Squarespace).

Any funny publishing stories?

Aside from some really terrible submissions, not really. I do have fun with the work, though. I think a lot of funny stories come from mistakes and I probably don't see the funny side.

Did you have any work experience in the publishing industry before you started your press? If yes, how did this inform your work? If no, how did you learn your craft?

None whatsoever. I learned by reading books and making mistakes in my own practice. I've made a lot of them and you learn because people point them out and they're that embarrassing. Also, other editors, authors, contributors, friends, have all helped speed up the learning. Alec Newman at KFS Press will occasionally get a barrage of messages from me and he's been very giving with his time.

How have you seen the independent publishing industry change since you started publishing?

I think while HVTN moved away from print-on-demand, more publishers moved towards it, which I find interesting. We had a bad experience doing it through Amazon and given Amazon is the bane of small publishers (and evil in other ways), I don't like seeing the small press world submit to it. Often under the guise of selling 'at-cost',(it's not sold at cost because Amazon keeps its profit margin - it's just the publisher sacrificing theirs), but it's really tough to stump up money for a print run, and Amazon's print on demand does remove a big obstacle for people who want to share the work they like. Ingram and Lightning Source I haven't myself used, but I know a couple of publishers who have and they seem to be good print-on-demand options. Although, I understand there are a couple of associated costs that aren't the case with Amazon (I could have that wrong). So yeah, I find the print-on-demand question interesting, particularly when it concerns Amazon.

What advice would you give someone interested in starting their own press?

Do it through print-on-demand or through hand-made chapbooks, in a limited run or PDFs - however you can do it. It's the sort of thing you can put off forever and you'll still make mistakes when you start so, if you can, just do it. There are low-cost ways of running a press (Dostoevsky Wannabee, Hesterglock, Zarf) are all good examples of how it can be done. The workload is tough, so ask someone who shares your interests to come on board. Don't do it if you think it will make you money, or if you think it will help your poetry or help you network. Those things are fine to have in the back of your mind but the priority has to be sharing/platforming interesting work that might not find a home elsewhere. Otherwise you'll burn out. You'll probably burn out anyway.

Louise Walters Books

In conversation with Louise Walters: writer, editor and publisher.

Louise Walters founded her small press in 2017. She lives in Northamptonshire.

Web: www.louisewaltersbooks.co.uk
Twitter: @LouiseWalters12

How many people are in your team, either paid or voluntary, and how do you divide your roles?

Just two. Me, and my "intern" Billie, who helps me with a bit of admin and proofreading. As I work from home, she "interns" remotely, but it's helping her get a bit of experience in publishing, and she helps me, so it works well.

What genre of books primarily do you publish and how many a year on average?

I publish literary/literary-commercial fiction for adult readers, currently up to four titles a year, one per season.

When did your press open for business and what was your first year like?

I opened in 2017 and the first year was very exciting, finding four authors and their wonderful novels.

What are the most rewarding things about running a small press?

Editing fabulous writers. It's my favourite part of the publishing process.

What are the most challenging things about running a small press?

Not having enough money to market my books; lack of sales! And not quite reaching the magical 50 reviews on Amazon...

What do you take into consideration when considering manuscripts and how do you compile your season of publishing (if this is curated in any way?)

I look for excellent writing; everything has to be in place; not perfect, but the novel must be well written. I look for very talented authors.

Do you advertise manuscript submissions? If not, how do you approach authors or agents? If you do, how do you spread the word and how many manuscripts do you expect to receive in a typical reading period?

I have a submissions page on my website. I recently closed to subs for a few months, as my schedule up to the end of 2020 is full. I'm about to re-open again as I am now looking for titles to publish in 2021. I get a handful of submissions per week... not many compared to bigger publishers, but it's all relative, and when you're basically a one-woman band, even a few submissions can be time-consuming.

What does a typical book marketing plan look like for you?

Several months ahead of publication I plan blogs and book shop appearances; I send out early review copies about six months before publication date; and I contact indie bookshops, and the chains, requesting they stock the books. Mixed results here! I offer giveways and competitions; and keep my website updated with the latest news. I send out newsletters and offer Supporter subscriptions - four books a year, invites to book launches, that kind of thing.

How do you continue to build your brand within a busy market?

I try to be authentic; I engage a lot on Twitter with anybody and everybody bookish; readers seem to like the whole indie publisher ethic so I try to engage and be social... it is SOCIAL media after all...

What parts of the publishing process do you do in-house and which do you outsource?

I project manage the publication process of each of my titles, and I edit and proofread. I outsource cover design, copy editing and typesetting/ebook conversion.

Did you have any work experience in the publishing industry before you started your press? If yes, how did this inform your work? If no, how did you learn your craft?

No work experience, but I was a trade published author, then a self-published author, and those processes taught me quite a lot. Since starting my indie press proper, I've taught myself all sorts of things, and I'm learning all the time.

How have you seen the independent publishing industry change since you started publishing?

I think there is a groundswell of support for indie presses in recent times; the smaller publishers with no money take all the big risks... the bigger publishers play it too safe and as a result publish a lot of mediocre stuff. Not all of what they publish is mediocre, of course - but there is too much of it.

If you don't mind disclosing money, what is your annual turnover?

About zero! I am running at a loss and make ends meet by doing editorial critiques and reports on a freelance basis. It's a real struggle and I may have to stop publishing, if only for a year or two, if sales don't pick up. It's quite the worry.

What advice would you give someone interested in starting their own press?

Be prepared to be skint but fulfilled. Be prepared for more work than you imagined, and expect to burn the candle at both ends. Do it as a hobby if you can, at least to begin with, and keep your day job. It's very difficult to make money in books.

Newfound Journal

In conversation with Laura Eppinger, managing editor and Levis Keltner, editor-in-chief.

They say: "We're a nonprofit publisher based in Austin, TX. Our work explores how place shapes identity, imagination, and understanding." Website: newfound.org

How many people are in your team, either paid or voluntary, and how do you divide your roles?

We are 100% driven by volunteer work. Levis Keltner is the editor-in-chief for Newfound projects (the journal and chapbook press) and president of the non-profit, and Laura Eppinger is the managing editor of Newfound Journal.

The journal publishes the following genres: Fiction, Creative Nonfiction, Poetry, Translation, Interview, Visual Arts, Flash Fiction, Creative Nonfiction, and Reviews. Each section has its own editor, and that editor works with a team of readers - usually between two and five folks. We have copy editors who edit for style in our journal and chapbook publications.

The chapbook press is overseen by Levis. The winners of the Gloria Anzaldúa Poetry Prize and Newfound Prose Prize are determined by a team of panellists and a different judge for each prize.

The organisation as a whole is lucky to have a director of public relations who manages promotion and social media. We are a 501(c)(3) non-profit and report to a board of directors.

What genre of books primarily do you publish and how many a year on average?

The press and the journal are guided by place-based enquiry. We publish work that explores how place shapes identity, imagination and understanding. The chapbook press runs two contests and one open call for submissions annually.

The Anzaldúa Poetry Prize proudly honours poet, writer, and cultural theorist, Gloria E. Anzaldúa. Anzaldúa's work highlights how one's place in the world is at once geographical, geopolitical, psychological, mythological, spiritual, and linguistic. She is well known for her book of prose and poetry, "Borderlands/La Frontera: The New Mestiza," which draws on her experience as a Chicana/ Tejana/lesbian/feminist activist - a revolutionary and inspirational work that continues to be so.

The Gloria E. Anzaldúa Poetry Prize is awarded annually, in conjunction with the Anzaldúa Literary Trust, to a poet whose work explores how place shapes identity, imagination, and understanding. Special attention is given to poems that exhibit multiple vectors of thinking: artistic, theoretical, and social, which is to say, political. One winner receives $1,000, twenty-five copies, and a royalties contract option.

We run an open call for poetry chapbooks in the month of December only, with no submission fee but also no prize awarded. Newfound accepts unsolicited chapbook-length manuscripts from writers who have not yet published a full-length book. Our open submission period aims to advance the careers of emerging writers by printing their work in beautiful, hand-bound editions. Submissions are open to finalists, but not winners of Newfound prizes. One chapbook per year is selected by Newfound staff.

Newfound also runs a prose prize chapbook contest, one of the few of its kind. The Newfound Prose Prize is awarded annually to a chapbook-length work of exceptional fiction or creative non-fiction. The work may be in the form of a long story or essay or a collection of short pieces (60 pages max). Other than the page limit, the only formal requirement is that some aspect of the work must inform or explore how place shapes identity, imagination, and understanding. One winner receives $500, twenty-five copies, and a royalties contract option.

When did your press open for business, and what was your first year like?

Newfound opened in 2013, like so many other budding literary endeavours, as an online journal. Since, we've expanded steadily. We achieved non-profit status in 2013 and had our first print edition the year later, followed by the Anzladúa Prize. In 2020, we'll start paying journal contributors. The first years are difficult due to the lack of capital. Even literary dreams take money. We've been lucky in that we understood from the start that both strong values and economic savvy were required to found a sustainable organisation.

What are the most rewarding things about running a small press?

Laura says: I work full-time in a university's agriculture department. I do not interact with other writers in my daily life, but having a writing community is very important to me. I enjoy working with our staff to put the journal together and to uplift the voices of the writers we publish. Newfound Journal is a labour of love and I am grateful to every member of our team for what they give. **Levis says:** Watching writers we've published gain notoriety and be celebrated by the literary community. All the work is worth those moments our writers express feeling appreciated, understood, and supported.

What are the most challenging things about running a small press?

Laura says: I wish we could pay our staff! I am always mindful that our readers, editors, and team members have work, families, other communities, and their own writing and publishing priorities. I never want volunteering for the journal to take away from one's own writing goals, though of course this happens. Sometimes folks who are a great fit have to step away from Newfound because of lack of time, and I always respect and understand that. Sometimes it feels like the turnover is high for our staff - life happens! Securing long-term funding for the journal is a goal of mine, which I keep putting off due to lack of time.

What do you take into consideration when considering manuscripts and how do you compile your season of publishing (if this is curated in any way?)

We prioritise emerging and underrepresented voices and hope our chapbooks propel writers in their careers.
We take the guidelines for the chapbook prizes very seriously. For example, for the Anzaldúa Poetry Prize, the panellists and judge are given a set of guidelines, designed largely by poet, educator, and activist Nico Amador, with feedback from Newfound volunteers. When shortlisting manuscripts for the prize, panellists are asked to consider: Does it explore the theme of place? Does the work honour the legacy of Anzaldúa as a groundbreaking and revolutionary cultural theorist, writing from a marginalized experience as a feminist, Chicana, lesbian activist? Is the manuscript in conversation with political forces, not simply in their naming, but in a new kind of engagement? How might each author benefit from the prize money, chapbook publication, and subsequent media attention? The Newfound Prose Prize is judged similarly. For our open call for poetry chapbooks, we only accept work by writers that have not yet published a full-length book.

Do you advertise manuscript submissions? If not, how do you approach authors or agents? If you do, how do you spread the word and how many manuscripts do you expect to receive in a typical reading period?

We advertise chapbook submission periods on Twitter, Facebook (both our own and call for submission pages), Submittable, Poets & Writers, Duotrope, our mailing list, and elsewhere. Manuscripts received range from 120-300 per category and are steadily growing.

What does a typical book marketing plan look like for you?

Our marketing plan grows with each release. There aren't a lot of venues to celebrate chapbook releases, so it's been exciting to build literary relationships to make that bandwidth. Currently, each chapbook is released roughly a year after acceptance. That gives us time to get ARCs out for blurbs, and those promo materials to potential reviewers, interviewers, and bookstores so that by pre-order, buzz about the chapbook drives sales.

How do you continue to build your brand within a busy market?

There are a lot of chapbook prizes, but not many dedicated chapbook presses out there. We set ourselves ahead of the pack by practising artful, handbound bookmaking with the engine of traditional book publisher. From object to content, when you buy a Newfound chapbook, you know you're reading something fresh and unforgettable.

What parts of the publishing process do you do in-house and which do you outsource?

We outsource the chapbook cover art and interior design to artist LK James, and printing to a local printer. All other work is done in-house.

Did you have any work experience in the publishing industry before you started your press? If yes, how did this inform your work? If no, how did you learn your craft?

Levis says: I worked as the web editor for an MFA online journal for two years. I learned that though MFA journals generally have more resources than independent publishers, the high turnover from year to year makes strategic planning, and therefore mindful change and growth, nearly impossible. I have mostly learned how to do Newfound by picking the brains of more established presses and by failing better.

How have you seen the independent publishing industry change since you started publishing?

There are more and more journals running chapbook prizes in an attempt to gain capital to fund their literary projects. A similar trend has happened with submission fees.

If you don't mind disclosing money, what is your annual turnover?

As a federal non-profit, all our 1099s are publicly disclosed from our website. Last year, we reached ~$8,000 in total support, which continues to increase annually.

What advice would you give someone interested
in starting their own press?

*"Consider why you need to start a new
press instead of joining an existing one
that would thrive from your voice and
talents."*

Broken Sleep Books

In conversation with Aaron Kent, Editor

Website: www.brokensleepbooks.com

Twitter: @BrokenSleep

They say... *"Broken Sleep Books is dedicated to works that transcend the page, and are more than just poets writing poetry. We believe the greatest pieces of writing exist outside of expectation, and are written with more than the act of writing in mind.*

We are particularly devoted to minimalist cover designs (such as the wonderful books by presses like Little Island), and wish to encourage more working-class writers, non-binary, and BAME writers to submit. Politically we are left-leaning, and we have no interest in misogynists, racist, sexists, the alt-right, or dickheads in general. Our interests lie in the works of J H Prynne, Anne Carson, Jorie Graham, Kim Addonizio, Edwin Brock, and Haruki Murakami."

How many people are in your team, either paid or voluntary, and how do you divide your roles?

There are only two of us running Broken Sleep Books, and primarily I do the majority of the work. I asked Charlie Baylis to work alongside as an assistant editor, and originally he was quite involved with the editing process, but recently he has been busy with his wonderful new journal Anthropocene (check it out!), and I haven't really gone to him much. Charlie still helps by writing the blurbs (not a strong point of mine, but he's great at it), and he helps by advising on submissions, which means I can have a discussion and debate about new manuscripts. I design the covers, typeset the books, communicate with authors, run social media, and all the other bits that come with running a small press. I do it all without making any money, and any money taken by the press means I'm working well below minimum wage. I teach English as a day job, and run Broken Sleep Books because I love publishing, and want to get the work of great writers out into the world, not because I want to make money. Though a dream would be to run it as a full-time job.

What genre of books primarily do you publish and how many a year on average?

I primarily publish poetry pamphlets, but have published a couple of poetry collections. I aim to publish two a month, one in the middle of the month, one at the end. I'd love to eventually branch out into essays and fiction, but for the time being the focus is entirely on poetry.

When did your press open for business and what was your first year like?

I began taking submissions at the start of 2018, after I tweeted that I'd be happy to take a look at anybody's manuscript for free to give out advice. I read Chris Kerr's Citidyll as part of that and liked it so much I wanted to publish it. The original idea was to publish pamphlets in cassette cases, handbound, miniature - and to publish collections in VHS cases, again handbound. The problem became that it was too restrictive, difficult to get right, meant the work would be extremely limited, and would mean I couldn't get poetry I loved out into as many hands as possible. So I released Chris' book in the cassette format, and then pivoted to the current style of 5x8 books. I was so happy with how well received Broken Sleep was in its first year, and that momentum has picked up in the second year.

What are the most rewarding things about running a small press?

I love it when authors respond with excitement at being accepted, that moment of joy in which they have a path to getting their work into the world is such a great feeling. I also love when great poets I've published go on to release books with other presses – I will always support poets I've published, and am always so proud of the work they go on to do.

What are the most challenging things about running a small press?

Trying to schedule everything to line up, newsletters, release dates, author copies, general sales, etc. I have spreadsheets to keep it all on track, but it can be quite time-consuming, and stresses me when one detail slips. I also have InDesign on my laptop, and my work PC, but they are different versions and the files aren't cross-compatible, so it takes a concerted effort to make sure I'm working on the right proof. I am about to upgrade to make it cross-compatible though.

What do you take into consideration when considering manuscripts and how do you compile your season of publishing (if this is curated in any way?)

I genuinely just want to publish work I love. I don't care if the poet has been published by the Guardian, PN Review, The Poetry Review, or whether this is their first attempt at submitting anywhere. If I love it, I'll publish it. I aimed to take submissions for six more pamphlets at the start of the year, and took on 12, because there were so many I just couldn't say no to. I try to curate with regards to how much work the poet feels they need to put in (a manuscript doesn't have to be finished for me to accept it based on its potential), and I work with the writer to determine the best date of release available for them and Broken Sleep.

Do you advertise manuscript submissions? If not, how do you approach authors or agents? If you do, how do you spread the word and how many manuscripts do you expect to receive in a typical reading period?

We advertise on our website (brokensleepbooks.com) and via Twitter (@BrokenSleep), but we only have one reading period a year (average so far over two years). Otherwise, I do approach poets whose work I love, not to ask them to publish with us, but just to tell them I adore their work, and if they ever wanted to submit, Broken Sleep would always be open to them. This was the case recently with Eva Griffin, who posted a poem of hers on Twitter that I adored, I told her I'd always be open to submissions from her, and a couple of months later she sent a pamphlet manuscript that is now due for release in December. We get a lot of submissions during a reading period – our first call out received 50 or so, but the second call out received almost ten a day in just two weeks.

What does a typical book marketing plan look like for you?

Broken Sleep doesn't have the funds to run whole marketing plans, so the focus is on social media and newsletters. We have so many visitors to the website daily that I'm confident in how we run. I always wanted Broken Sleep to be fairly minimal in its approach, hence the minimalist covers, so the idea is to be more personable on Twitter and allow the books to speak for themselves. I have been making more of an effort to engage via social media too.

How do you continue to build your brand within a busy market?

Consistency. I want people to see a cover and know it's Broken Sleep, or to buy our books knowing how consistent the quality of work is.

What parts of the publishing process do you do in-house and which do you outsource?

I design the covers on Adobe Photoshop, and typeset on Adobe InDesign, and we currently use KDP to publish. But I recently bought an old letterpress (thanks to some wonderful donations from supporters of Broken Sleep), which I will be refurbishing, and am planning on handpressing, handbinding limited runs of certain pamphlets. The books chosen will still be mass available, but there will be secondary limited versions of them for sale too, at a higher price.

Did you have any work experience in the publishing industry before you started your press? If yes, how did this inform your work? If no, how did you learn your craft?

I started a press a few years back – I Came Here Looking For a Fight – and released a couple of books through that, but I couldn't commit like I wanted to, and I was fairly amateurish (though still proud of the work produced). Knowing where I went wrong with ICHLFAF meant I knew what to change with BSB. I've never worked in publishing, but have had 7 pamphlets published all by different presses, and seeing the different styles and methods helped me to really come to terms with what I wanted to publish. Trial and error is key, and poets telling me what they'd like changed, helps me to see new ways of doing things. When I released Sarah Cave's An Arbitrary Line, she was really helpful in telling me about how to get the margins, and type right, as she runs the excellent Guillemot Press with Luke Thompson.

How have you seen the independent publishing industry change since you started publishing?

I've only been publishing with Broken Sleep for 18 months, and I wasn't really connected to the industry with I Came Here Looking For A Fight – so I haven't really noticed much. I think Twitter has become quite useful, and I originally began talking about BSB as a 'we', but now have gone to 'I' because it's so personal to me. I think the industry is way too committed to London, but that's not just publishing-specific, most industries are. I feel like I'm not part of a community because the community exists in London.

What advice would you give someone interested in starting their own press?

"Just do it. Really. You can spend forever saying that you would if... but you may as well just do it and learn along the way. I'm a teacher and I tell my students that you don't pass or fail, you pass or learn."

Ghost City Press

In Conversation with Kevin Bertolero, Founding Editor

Ghost City Press is an independent publishing house based out of Syracuse, NY

Kevin Bertolero is the founding editor of Ghost City Press. His work was long-listed for the 2018 Peach Gold Prize and his poems and essays have been published in Maudlin House, PNK PRL, Reality Beach, OUT/CAST, Tenderness Lit, Sea Foam Mag, and elsewhere. He tweets @KevinBertolero.

How many people are in your team, both paid and voluntary, and how do you divide your roles?

This has fluctuated over the years. We've had at any given point one person (just me) or up to six or seven people. Editors get busy, and the job doesn't pay very much. It's truly a labor of love to make this work, but it definitely is work. A lot of time and energy go into producing journals and books, and it's a collaborative process, which - depending on availability - can stretch out projects for even longer periods of time. It takes planning, but I think with a smaller, more focused team, we're able to accomplish more in a shorter period of time, even if that small team changes for each project.

When did your press open for business and what was your first year like?

I remember thinking about starting Ghost City back in the summer of 2013. I had been making small chapbooks for my own work, and I was doing a few for my friends. I thought, why can't we just mass produce these and find an audience for them? So that's what we did. My friend Deirdre Coyle talked me into it while we were having lunch one day, so I started doing research. I remember sitting in a coffee shop with my friend Kyla Bills, planning everything out. That feels like so long ago. The first year for us was pretty slow and very controlled, actually. We wanted to make sure that we could do this the right (legal) way, that it wouldn't be cost prohibitive, and that we could actually produce nice books of poetry. We took it one collection at a time until we felt comfortable with the process. It wasn't until we started the Summer Series in 2016 that we seemed to find our audience, though.

What are the most rewarding things about running a small press?

Seeing the reactions of our writers is without a doubt the most rewarding part of this process. I continually forget what it feels like to hold your book in your hands for the first time, and the excitement of seeing other people holding your book and reading it and sharing it on social media. There's nothing like it, and as a publisher I get to do that over and over again. Especially with the Summer Series, I get to experience that joy almost every single day for three months straight. It's invigorating as a publisher and it's a nice reminder of why we do what we do.

What are the most challenging things about running a small press?

Communication and coordination. Trying to keep projects on track is so difficult, whether we're waiting for edits and revisions on a manuscript, final changes to jacket art, making sure the layout looks good, making sure everything is sent to the printer on time... it's a lot of small deadlines to keep track of and a lot of emails to respond to. Making sure that the product we're producing is marketable, but also making sure it's true to the writers' vision is very important to us.

What do you take into consideration when considering manuscripts and how do you compile your season of publishing (if this is curated in any way?)

This is easy. If I like it and want to read it, I'll publish it. I always have a small wish-list of writers I'd like to work with, whether I've read their other books or found their poems published in other journals, I keep track. Most of the time I'll reach out to them directly, and other times, as if by chance, they'll contact me first. I also love working with writers on successive projects, because we're able to develop a more nuanced approach to this process the second or third time around. I also love the writers who are willing to push the boundaries of what these books can look like. Right now, we're working on a curated anthology of art and poetry inspired by art history and architectural theory. There's not going to be anything else like it and that's so exciting to me, and it's so much fun to work on.

What does a typical book marketing plan look like for you?

We try our best to target the writers' home markets. These seem to be the best places to sell these books, and it really helps to cement our writers as notable figures within their own communities. It's hard to find a broad audience on the internet when there is so much other work to compete with. We've found our biggest audience on Twitter, but we also go to book fairs across the east coast and we try to sell books in person as often as we can. We also target specific regional bookstores for each release. It's different for every title we put out, but it's a process we've refined over the past few years. We're never going to have the kind of distribution or attention that a press like Graywolf or Copper Canyon has, so we do our own thing and we do it well.

How do you continue to build your brand within a busy market?

I think the tradition of our Summer Micro-Chap Series has really helped to give us a broader audience and establish a unique place for us to exist within this market. Other presses publish micro-chaps, sure, but we have such an impressively curated series every year that it's more noticeable, I guess. Each year, we've had more and more subscribers and downloads and the number of donations we've received has increased as well. Because the market is so overcrowded, it's tough to make any money from your work these days, but with the Summer Series we're able to help our writers out a little bit more, and that's the goal really.

What parts of the publishing process do you do in-house and which do you outsource?

The only parts of this process which are outsourced are cover design and printing. We occasionally do jacket design work in-house, and all of our regular chapbooks are handmade, printed and bound in-house. But it's not uncommon for our writers to have friends who are willing to create beautiful cover art for their projects, and we encourage that. We've also been working with the same printing company for the past five years, and they've done a beautiful job with all of our paperback books.

Any funny publishing stories?

It's not funny necessarily, but it's just interesting who you can meet through the publishing process. We've been able to establish good relationships with writers, editors, artists, other presses, bookstores, venues, and numerous others since we started Ghost City. That's been the best thing about this whole process. I've personally made some great friends (some of whom I've never met in person), and it's brought new projects to life and lead to different opportunities. For that I am very grateful.

Queen of Swords Press

In Conversation with Catherine Lundoff, Publisher

Queen of Swords is an independent small press specializing in swashbuckling tales of derring-do, bold new adventures in time and space, mysterious stories of the occult and arcane and fantastical tales of people and lands far and near.

Catherine Lundoff is an award-winning writer, editor and publisher from Minneapolis where she lives with her wife and the cats who own them. She is the author of over 100 published short stories and essays and nine books, including Silver Moon, Out of This World: Queer Speculative Fiction Stories and Unfinished Business: Tales of the Dark Fantastic. She has also edited or co-edited three anthologies including the multi-genre pirate anthology, Scourge of the Seas of Time (and Space). In addition, she is the publisher at Queen of Swords Press, a genre fiction publisher specializing in fiction from out of this world. Websites: www.catherinelundoff.net and www.queenofswordspress.com

How many people are in your team, both paid and voluntary, and how do you divide your roles?

I have a part-time publishing assistant who handles the Queen of Swords Press newsletter, maintains some of our social media, reviews submissions and assists on copyediting, marketing work and event sales. I handle the developmental editing, all the marketing, the bookkeeping, the events sales, the actual production of books and so forth. No one works for free, except me, sort of.

What genre of books primarily do you publish and how many a year on average?

We have published fantasy, steampunk, science fiction romance, horror, dark fantasy and short fiction so far. Our first year, we published 4 books, 3 the second and 2 the third. I'm working on getting back up to 3 in 2020.

When did your press open for business and what was your first year like?

We published our first title in January 2017. The first year, I only published my backlist titles because I knew I had to learn more about distribution and marketing and I didn't want to "practice" on other people's work. I had and still do have a fulltime job and had no publishing assistant at the time but decided to publish four books, so it was kind of nuts! I did all my own marketing and sales on top of that. So, on the one hand, I can say that I learned a bunch about everything from book formatting to writing ad copy that first year, but on the other, I could have been a lot more realistic and efficient about it.

What are the most rewarding things about running a small press?

The opportunity to see a new book come together, the chance to publish writers, getting to see a reader discover a new book that you've published, one that you're really excited about. It's an incredible learning experience, one that I'm (generally) glad that I tackled.

What are the most challenging things about running a small press?

Finances, marketing on a small budget and keeping a thousand things in motion while working at a day job and having other commitments. I suspect it would be somewhat easier if I wasn't also writing, but I'm certainly not prepared to give that up. So there's factoring in writing time and finding energy for that on top of all the other stuff. The absolute hardest parts are getting people to notice you and be willing to check out your books when the world feels like it's coming apart around us.

What do you take into consideration when considering manuscripts and how do you compile your season of publishing (if this is curated in any way?)

I have to feel passionate about everything I publish because we're such a small operation and I handle most of the sales and marketing. What I consider a good fit for us to publish can be boiled down to the following: Is it in a genre that we intend to publish in or are already publishing in? Do I love it? Could I sell it? Is this by an author or authors that I can work with over the long term? I think a lot of small press publishers don't consider this last factor and I think it's an important one. A good working relationship is essential to everyone's success, especially for a contract that can last up to five years. I'm trying to get better at scheduling book releases - most of my releases have been event-driven, in the sense that I want to put the book out in time for some specific marketing opportunity like a StoryBundle or a convention. I'm working on longer term planning for the next couple of years now though and we'll see how that goes. I'm a pantser by nature so learning to plan like that can sometimes be a challenge.

Do you advertise manuscript submissions? If not, how do you approach authors or agents? If you do, how do you spread the word and how many manuscripts do you expect to receive in a typical reading period?

The two books that I published by Alex Acks were solicited by invitation, as is A.J. Fitzwater's forthcoming collection in 2020. We just ended our first open manuscript submissions period. I got 15 submissions (synopsis plus three chapters) and 3 or 4 queries with supporting materials. The submissions window was 6 weeks long and was advertised on all our social media and our newsletter, as well as in several marketing and writer's groups on Facebook. I requested two full manuscripts and am reading them now, for those curious. In contrast, my call for fantastical pirate stories went out to all the major market sites and resulted in 100 submissions from 14 countries.

We'll likely spread our next manuscript submissions call a bit further and that will probably happen next year. This year, I had a lot going on in my personal life and was concerned about keeping things at a level that my assistant and I could handle. I suspect that submissions will remain a combination of open submissions and invites for the foreseeable future.

Some of the lower numbers for our submissions window are also due to people just learning about the press. I think that will change organically as we grow. I haven't received any agented manuscripts yet, which is not surprising because Queen of Swords is not an advance-paying publisher at this point in time. I do hope to be eventually though.

What does a typical book marketing plan look like for you?

I build a press kit for each individual title and use that as the basis for announcements, press releases and soliciting reviewers. We have a reviewers list and I reach out to them first to see if they want to see a specific book; I do try to approach specific reviewers about specific titles that are in their wheelhouse. Then I build from there; ideally, I want each book to have a YouTube video of the author reading associated with it and several appearances (readings, conferences, guest blogs, podcasts, etc.) to support a book release. For example, I'm releasing a collection of my horror and dark fantastic fiction on October 1st, because Halloween celebrations start early in the U.S. I'll be doing 2 event book tables, a science fiction and fantasy convention with a full programming lineup, 2 release readings and a guest blog to support it. For a Spring release, like Wireless and More Steam-Powered Adventures by Alex Acks, we were able to get it included in StoryBundle's Pride Month Bundle and hosted a release party for it at WisCon, along with reviews, interviews and related publicity. My marketing philosophy is to ask until someone says, "No," then look for another option.

How do you continue to build your brand within a busy market?

It's an ongoing effort. Queen of Swords Press is, like my reading tastes, pretty eclectic. At the moment, I'm engaged in launching a new "Minis" series, which will feature single author collections of short speculative fiction, with all stories tied together thematically by character, world or genre. These will all be in the 40k word range, so about half the size of a standard trade paperback. I'm hoping to use to these to capture book buyers at festivals and other events that are attracted to a lower price point than I can put on my regular-sized titles as well as to use to these to convince readers to try new authors. I'm also looking at starting up an imprint for Minnesota and regional fantasy and horror authors. I also want to build toward publishing more fantasy, sf and horror with historical elements. Ultimately, I'm more interested in having a well-rounded catalogue of books that speak to a diverse readership than in having a single "brand," per se. Our brand is currently "Books Catherine likes".

What parts of the publishing process do you do in-house and which do you outsource?

I contract out some of the copyediting, all of the cover art and all the book design work for the print books. I also hire on help from time to time for marketing campaigns. I also have a webmaster who handles problems and big website updates and changes, a small business attorney and an accountant who does our taxes. I format the ebook editions myself using a program called Vellum, I write the marketing copy, create the ads, make the promotional materials, maintain the website, do the day to day bookkeeping, pay the bills, handle distribution and so forth.

Did you have any work experience in the publishing industry before you started your press? If yes, how did this inform your work? If no, how did you learn your craft?

I actually grew up in New York publishing – my mother worked for a couple of the big publishers for many years. I used to hang out in various offices as a kid, help out with small projects, model for textbooks and that sort of thing. I also have some background as a bookseller. Before I started the press, I spent a couple of years doing research, taking small business and copywriting classes, reading and talking to people about what they were doing. I have been traditionally published for many years so I knew what some of the small press publishing industry looked like before I embraced the idea of doing it myself.

How have you seen the independent publishing industry change since you started publishing?

Well, it's only been two and a half years. I think that the larger issues that impact the world economies and political situations certainly have an impact, as does publisher consolidation, the elimination of the midlist, the growth of Amazon and other factors all impact indie publishing as well. It's harder to get people to buy books and to pay attention to book marketing when everything is on fire all the time, literally and figuratively. I'm certainly not ready to give up yet though and I keep working on supporting good things as much as I can.

If you don't mind disclosing money, what is your annual turnover?

In 2017, I spent about $3900 and brought in around $3300 in sales. In 2018, I spent around $10,000 and brought in around $4700 in sales, which was obviously not sustainable. I haven't run all my numbers for this year yet, but I would say that it's running about $4000 in expenses and around $3300 in sales, so far. So sales are going up, but we're not breaking even yet. I'm funding the Press from my day job paycheck, as well as additional money from teaching writing classes, doing talks, our Patreon, etc. My immediate goal is to get to the point where the Press covers expenses and I don't have to subsidize it, then build up to paying myself.

What advice would you give someone interested in starting their own press?

Bear in mind that almost everything takes more time than you expect so always build in a buffer for time and money in case you need it. Other publishers and indie authors can be amazing friends and allies so look to build a network before you get started. Focus on what works for you in terms of books and marketing; you can always build out from there.

Neon Books

In Conversation with Krishan Coupland, Editor

Neon Books is a UK-based independent publisher, producing a small-number of carefully-selected chapbooks, pamphlets and other ephemera each year. It also publishes Neon, one of the longest-running independent literary magazines in the UK.
Twitter: https://twitter.com/Neon_Lit_Mag
Facebook: https://www.facebook.com/NeonBooksUK/

Krishan Coupland is a graduate from the University of East Anglia MA Creative Writing programme. His debut chapbook When You Lived Inside The Walls is available from Stonewood Press, and his short fiction appears in Ambit, Aesthetica and Litro. He has won the Manchester Fiction Prize, and the Bare Fiction Prize. He runs and edits Neon Literary Magazine. He is unduly pre-occupied with theme parks. His website is www.krishancoupland.co.uk.

How many people are in your team, both paid and voluntary, and how do you divide your roles?

For the most part it's just me, although I sometimes have voluntary help with reading submissions – which is amazingly helpful. That aside, I do everything from editorial work down to troubleshooting digital subscriptions.

What genre of books primarily do you publish and how many a year on average?

Neon Books publishes poetry. I publish one book per year, although this year (2019) I've instead been dedicating my energy to two unusual projects: The Liminal Residency and Poetry in Public, which I've worked on rather than publishing a book.

When did your press open for business and what was your first year like?

I started a literary magazine many years ago now – the press grew out of that. I found the work I received for the magazine inspiring, and wanted to be able to publish collections and chapbooks. It was around four years ago now that Neon Books published its first few chapbooks. That first year involved a lot of learning. Poetry chapbooks and novellas are difficult things to sell, but there were also some real high points that helped keep me going, including winning a Saboteur Award.

What are the most rewarding things about running a small press?

It's immensely rewarding when something I've helped publish really reaches someone. Every so often someone will send an email saying how much they enjoyed the magazine or one of the chapbooks, and it makes my day every time.

What are the most challenging things about running a small press?

Definitely finding the time to do everything that needs doing. I manage, but it's a constant juggling act, and a few things sometimes fall by the wayside. I'd love to have twice the number of hours in a day so that I could publish more stuff!

What do you take into consideration when considering manuscripts and how do you compile your season of publishing (if this is curated in any way?)

My main consideration when deciding to take a project

forward is whether I love it. If I don't love it, then I know I won't get behind it 100% and really push it out there. In order to want to publish something it really has to speak to me. Beyond that I look for projects that are about something. It's a hundred times easier to sell a poetry collection that has a strong central theme than one that you can only describe as "a collection of poetry".

Do you advertise manuscript submissions? If not, how do you approach authors or agents? If you do, how do you spread the word and how many manuscripts do you expect to receive in a typical reading period?

I run open calls for submissions, and advertise them in a few different places. I think most submissions come from word of mouth, though. During a typical submissions window I might receive two hundred submissions. Narrowing that down to just one project to take forward is always immensely difficult.

What does a typical book marketing plan look like for you?

As well as the usual business of seeking reviews, sending out copies to bookstores and libraries, and promoting the book on social media, I also look for opportunities to do unusual things with the text. This might be an amusing insert to send out with the magazine, an interactive promotional piece to publish online, or a video featuring the poet reading their work – anything that can grab some attention and give people a flavour of the book.

How do you continue to build your brand within a busy market?

The market is a busy one, but I'd much rather collaborate than compete. I enjoy doing advertising swaps with other publishers, curating resources for writers, and also staying in touch with writers after their work is published, to both promote their success and keep their book in the eyeline of buyers.

What parts of the publishing process do you do in-house and which do you outsource?

I do almost everything in house, although I sometimes outsource cover design.

Any funny publishing stories?

I've had people send along some very strange things – including whole boxes of already-published books, forged manuscripts ostensibly by long-dead famous literary figures, and 100,000 word Western epic novel trilogies. Some of it is lovely, though; one man sent along a poem about the process of submitting, which was warm, unexpected, and a joy to read, even if he didn't want to publish it!

Did you have any work experience in the publishing industry before you started your press? If yes, how did this inform your work? If no, how did you learn your craft?

I had no experience at all, and so worked things out as I went along. Lots of trial and error! Things were (and are) changing very rapidly in publishing, though, so there was always plenty of opportunity to stay ahead of the curve.

How have you seen the independent publishing industry change since you started publishing?

Hugely. It's hard to sum up the changes in a short paragraph because they've been so many and varied. Some things represent changes for the worse, but I'm a firm believer that things are also changing for the better in publishing too.

If you don't mind disclosing money, what is your annual turnover?

I don't have exact numbers, but suffice to say it's tiny. Neon Books really is a very small press!

What advice would you give someone interested in starting their own press?

"There's lots of practical stuff I would suggest, but the more useful intangible thing I would say is to have a really good grasp of what you want to put out there. Find something that isn't being published right now and define that as closely as you can before you get started. That'll really help down the road."

Mason Jar Press

In conversation with Michael, Managing Editor

Mason Jar Press has been publishing full-length books and limited-run chapbooks since 2014. The Press is dedicated to finding new and exciting work by writers that push the bounds of literary norms. While the work Mason Jar seeks to publish is meant to challenge status quos, both literary and culturally, it must also have significant merit in both those realms.

Michael B. Tager is a Baltimore-based writer and editor. He is the Managing Editor of Mason Jar Press, an independent publisher of high-quality books. Recent publications include Necessary Fiction, Hobart, Barrelhouse, and The Collagist, among others. He lives with his wife and cats, and is a part-time narwhal. Find out more at Michaelbtager.com.

How many people are in your team, both paid and voluntary, and how do you divide your roles?

We started out as Ian and Michael, as sort of a lark. That has grown to include other editors and podcast hosts. We assign duties based on our needs and strengths. Ian and Michael are terrible proofers and copyeditors, so Ashley came on board and gradually became the lead content editor. Briana is the web manager, Heather is the PR editor, Rachel and Taylor are readers and Celeste and Anthony are podcast hosts. Michael can now focus on managing and Ian can design/be the boss.

We all do some editing and reading, based on our interests, but focus on our main areas. All of our roles are voluntary: at this point, MJP pays our authors and writers who read at our events, and occasionally treats staff to dinners and beers. Hopefully someday we'll be able to pay, if only honorariums.

What genre of books primarily do you publish and how many a year on average?

We've been publishing 3-4 books a year and we're near our upper limit, for the moment. Maybe we'll expand in the future. We do fiction, non-fiction and poetry, with an eye toward the somewhat experimental. Genre isn't a barrier one way or the other, but a meld of experimental and literary is our focus.

When did your press open for business and what was your first year like?

The beginning of Mason Jar Press is a little nebulous, and there are different events that could theoretically mark the start. For our purposes, though, we generally consider the publication of three small chapbooks, collectively the *Pop Culture Collection*, by Michael as the beginning. Mike approached Ian to design the cover for the chapbooks which he was going to self publish. Ian liked the poems so much, though, and was already toying with the idea of starting a small press, that he asked Mike if he could publish the chapbooks under the Mason Jar Press name. The two found that they worked really well together, and shared a vision for what the press could be, so Mike stayed on and they started looking for other titles to publish.

The first person they approached was a local poet, Matthew Falk, who was crazy enough to agree to let them put out a chapbook of his poetry. It was an experiment to see if they could do it and to see if they enjoyed working together. The experiment was a success, so they kept on going.

That chapbook, and the one that followed — another poetry collection; this time by Stephen Zerance — were hand-sewn with a limited run of 100 copies. A lot was learned that first year, and Mason Jar was able to parlay the success of the chapbooks into a foray into perfect-bound, full-length titles with *Notes From My Phone* by Michelle Junot. Since

Michelle's, we've done more perfect-bound books, with Malka Older's ...and Other Disasters set to release in November and more currently in production.

What are the most rewarding things about running a small press?

We're putting art out into the world. What can be more rewarding than that?

What are the most challenging things about running a small press?

Time, energy. We all have full-time jobs, many of us have children. This happens in our in-between hours and it requires a lot of energy to do it all.

What do you take into consideration when considering manuscripts and how do you compile your season of publishing (if this is curated in any way?)

Our first consideration when approaching a manuscript is whether it sits well with Mason Jar's artistic goals and our catalogue as a whole. We love to see manuscripts that represent underrepresented voices, that maybe don't fit cleanly into one particular genre, or that are working to dismantle or reshape expectations. We also consider a manuscript's readiness for publication. While we sometimes extend an offer to an author whose manuscript needs extensive rewrites or expansion, we're typically looking for projects that are already there or there-adjacent. As a small press whose staff have day jobs, we don't always have the bandwidth to work on long term development projects, which is heartbreaking when we have to let a promising but incomplete project go, but it's simply not a realistic practice for us right now.

"We try to curate a healthy blend of works in fiction, non-fiction, and poetry to keep our catalogue from feeling too lopsided or stagnant, which is always on our minds when discussing future projects. Our core editors typically discuss how many projects we think we can carry over roughly a two-year span (usually two per calendar year, but sometimes three) and what types of projects we should bring in, and then those ideas are presented to the whole Mason Jar group where further brainstorming continues. A rough schedule is blocked out to accommodate the selection process, editing, and marketing for those projects that will be fine-tuned once the project eventually starts."

Do you advertise manuscript submissions? If not, how do you approach authors or agents? If you do, how do you spread the word and how many manuscripts do you expect to receive in a typical reading period?

We have open submissions and solicited manuscripts. It kind of depends on what we're interested in. In 2019, we had two manuscript open submission periods—for poetry and nonfiction—and one horror anthology that we advertised via social media (Twitter, Facebook, Instagram) as well as websites Duotrope and Entropy's Where to Submit. And then of course, there's word of mouth. We are usually open for a month or so and receive between 100 and 200 manuscripts. For short story anthologies, we receive more. We had to shut down horror subs after we hit 400. It was too much!

When we aren't doing open calls, we solicit people. All the members of Mason Jar get together for a meeting and we throw out what kinds of writing we want to see, what we've done recently and some authors we admire and would want to work with. Typically we've approached people we already know for solicitations, so it's not terribly hard to shoot them a quick email. People definitely say no, but they also say yes! And of course, we're always open for pitches. We say no to the vast majority but we do look at manuscripts sometimes. We said yes to one pitch in the last 4 years, to Dave Ring's *Broken Metropolis*. It seemed cool and he had a divine business plan.

What does a typical book marketing plan look like for you?

Ugh. Marketing. This is definitely the most challenging for us. We're all relatively smart people with advanced degrees and everything, but none of us were trained in marketing. It's why we've recently pulled a PR manager (Heather Rounds) on board to help us with this!

We have a multi-tiered approach to what we do. First, we get blurbs to advertise the book from a curated list of readers we generate with the author. And then we ask the author to put together a list of organizations (e.g. journals, radio stations, newspapers, colleges and universities they've attended, etc.) that they might have a connection to and we add it to our own list that we have. We send all those people standard press releases. Finally, we usually put together a reading tour to promote the book, based on the author's preferences and location. For Danny's tour of his book of poetry, *Continental Breakfast*, there was a multi-state reading with twenty-some stops.

And of course, social media. Our EIC runs the account and he's quite funny.

How do you continue to build your brand within a busy market?

We have focused on building our social media presence

over the past couple of years and continue to engage in literary events and programs to keep our name in people's minds and our books in their hands. We also rely on our work ethic and the relationships we foster with our authors to build our brand as a sharp, reliable, quirky little press. Our ultimate goal is to create good art with good people and to treat everyone and their work with respect, which tends to make our authors happy, which then tends to lead to our press being recommended to other authors and bookstores and agents, which builds our reach and following.

What parts of the publishing process do you do in-house and which do you outsource?

The vast majority of the process (reading, selecting works, editing, layout and cover design, marketing, and accounting) is completed by our core group. We do utilize an outside vendor, Spencer Printing, for printing our books, we recently started working with Small Press Distribution, and we will occasionally bring in outside readers to help work through submissions. We are not shy about asking for help when we need it, especially if we're surprised by a huge number of submissions or have a tricky legal or business question, but we like to keep all creative decisions in-house.

Did you have any work experience in the publishing industry before you started your press? If yes, how did this inform your work? If no, how did you learn your craft?

Most of us went to the University of Baltimore and got our MFA in creative writing and publishing. So we understood design and editing and the physical process of making a book, which was definitely a leg up. Ian and Michael, who founded Mason Jar, both had experience in lit journals and reading series as well. So they knew people and had a sort of base to begin with.

We were also acquainted with indie publishers and we pumped them for advice. Adam Robinson from Publishing Genius gave us a lot of good advice (get your accounting set up BEFORE you start was invaluable, for example). And the Barrelhouse/Hobarts folk had a wealth of knowledge as well. Even our colleagues at Ink Press Productions gave us tips on contracts and whatnot. That doesn't mean we haven't grown a LOT since then. We've learned a lot on the job, both obvious and not-so-obvious.

How have you seen the independent publishing industry change since you started publishing?

We've seen a bunch of journals and presses end in the past couple of years for a variety of reasons. A lot of them seem to have just run their course over a period of years and decided to call it quits. We understand that! It's a lot of work for little money and after a while, there's only so much to give. Some places didn't know how to manage money and either ran out of it or didn't pay their authors and ran afoul of that. I mean, come on. Pay your authors, people!

What advice would you give someone interested in starting their own press?

1)   *Ask your friends in the business for help. Ask them to tell you how to do things, what you don't know that you don't know. Most of us were helped by someone else along the way and we want to give back.*

2)   *Start small. Here at MJP, we did a trial run with a friend who we were comfortable with (and who knew we were experimenting on them). When that was successful, we scaffolded a little and applied lessons learned. And we kept on building: more books a year, more ambitious projects, non-local authors.*

Indigo Dreams

In conversation with co-director, Ronnie Goodyer

Indigo Dreams is run by poets Ronnie Goodyer and partner Dawn Bauling. They have many collections to their names and next year will be publishing a joint collection which will be launched at the Cheltenham Poetry Festival in April 2020. Ronnie is also Poet-in-Residence for animal welfare charity, The League Against Cruel Sports.

How many people are in your team, both paid and voluntary, and how do you divide your roles?

There are two people in our team, myself and Dawn Bauling. Regarding poetry collections: Dawn looks after the proofing process and review copies, plus mail order sales. I handle events and social media, covers, setting books for print, arranging final pre-publication details with author, registration of titles for publication with Nielsen's and our distributor, ordering of books from printers. I also create the author web pages on our site. Many other subsidiary items in relation to what's already stated. We both look after the demands of welfare for rescue dog, Mist the Merle – company collie!

Regarding our magazines: Dawn is editor of *Sarasvati* and *The Dawntreader* quarterlies. I am editor of *Reach Poetry* monthly. I look after the cover designs – from Dawn's ideas if for her mags. We each select content for inclusion and typesetting in our respective magazines. Again, I prepare all for printing and print ordering. Dawn also looks after the company accounts, which is better for all concerned, really...

When did your press open for business and what was your first year like?

Indigo Dreams was created back in 2005. I was the sole proprietor (it became Limited Company 2010). It mainly focused on the long-running monthly poetry magazine *Reach*. It was an enjoyable year because it was laid-back (like me) and poetry filled my working days. It introduced the (now quarterly) magazine *The Dawntreader* in 2007. That had themes of pantheistic, landscape, myth, nature, legend, spirituality and love / concern for the environment. It is now edited by Dawn and is our largest selling magazine, overtaking my painstakingly prepared 250+ issue 20+ year Reach Poetry. Tch....

What are the most rewarding things about running a small press?

The fact that, within our own financial and time constraints, we can publish what and who we like. We have a great reputation for our friendly and efficient relationship with our poets and that is really important to us. Our motto is *Pleasure not Pressure*. Publishing someone's collection, pamphlet or even single poem is a wonderful experience and it should be enjoyed. It's safe to say our poets do! We've built a tremendous stable of poets, from first-time publication to experienced. Incidentally, all our books and magazines are print form only. The day to day contact is as enjoyable today as many years ago. We love our poets!

It also seems (and is) very personally rewarding when you win things. When we entered the Saboteur Awards we did fairly well. We were Runner-up (second place) in the Most Innovative Publisher category 2016 and 2018 and won in 2017. That was a good night! The two of us were also the first ever joint winners of the Ted Slade Award. Whoop!

Tell us about the Ted Slade Award.

This was established in 2005. It is given *"to a person, or persons, who has given their time and energies over an extended period to ensuring the continuance and development of poetry.*

This will include people who have kept poetry as a presence in an area or community. Those who have pursued a poetic vision through a magazine or regular reading events. Those who have developed other media to explore its poetic use or have published poets who could not have otherwise found an outlet for their work."

The two of us were delighted to be the first joint recipients, following wonderful people like Sally Evans, Michael Horovitz, Peter Finch and Geoff Stevens (one of our competitions is in his honour and memory). Jim Bennett of Poetry Kit, who organises the award wrote: *"Ronnie and Dawn are stalwarts of poetry publishing and have given first publication to many poets through magazines, collections and pamphlets and are always forthcoming with help and advice. It is a great pleasure for me to give this award to our first joint recipients."* Needless to say, we were rather pleased and birds fled from Cookworthy Forest (where we live) at the sound of merry-making and popping corks.

What are the most challenging things about running a small press?

Ensuring that you keep within your physical work capacity and not over commit to too many publications or projects. We don't do stress – we try to keep to our own Pleasure not Pressure ethic! Also ensuring that the financial aspect isn't stretched. We rely on physical sales and promotions to keep going, and we're managing to do that quite well so far.

What do you take into consideration when considering manuscripts and how do you compile your season of publishing (if this is curated in any way?)

When reviewing one of our books, the Morning Star quoted Indigo Dreams as one of four *'shining examples'* of presses who *'keep the doors open for different kinds of voices and experiences.'*

We look for submissions that engage immediately and go on to maintain that interest - not with the exhibitionism of a lap-dancer, but with the subtle surprise of spice in a meal, one that leaves a lingering taste; a unique style with few wasted words, well written and well constructed. *"Do I need this word, this explanation?"* is a good question to keep asking. It must be the final version of the book that we are reading, dressed in its Sunday best clothes. There is no point in submitting a first draft – and we have been surprised how many did until we emphasised the point. Poetry should show knowledge of the form and avoidance of cliché. If it's a familiar subject, express it uniquely. We like 'uniqueness'!

In addition to the presentation qualities mentioned, we like to see authors that are willing to engage in the selling process to maximise sales, though this really should be second nature. A book is a joint journey with each side knowing their responsibilities.

Dawn and I consider our options for the following year, quantity and likely income. We open each September for collection and pamphlet submissions. We can only accept some 10% of those we enjoy. The worst part is always letting people down, those who in our opinion deserve to be published. The best part is advising those who are joining our #indigopoets.

Currently we have some 4,500 books in stock at our distributor, and have published about 250 poets in collections. If you add poets in our magazines its well into four figures. Our magazine Reach Poetry has paid out £12,700 in prize money to poets. Not sure it's relevant to this section but, hey, that pretty good isn't it.

We also run competitions for publication throughout the year. Submissions to our three magazines never close. One of these, Sarasvati, gives a showcase of 4 pages or so to each of the poets selected.

What does a typical book marketing plan for you?

We send Information Sheets to selected trade outlets, review copies to poetry magazines, social media campaigns for each title. We promote them in any way we can. By far the majority of sales are from the individual poets. They each have a full page on our website that showcases several poems from the collection. We are aware of their sales / promo plan and promo on social media and monthly newsletter, Indigo News. We also have Indigo Showcases where Indigo poets join forces for readings and tours.

How do you continue to build your brand within a busy market?

It is indeed a busy market. Social media has enabled a huge number of publishers to spring up and flourish. We are known for high product production levels and (are told) we are highly regarded in poetry circles, which is nice. We maintain a visible presence on FB and TW, and speak as we believe. When you have a passion for poetry and our poets, it comes across as such. We are also blessed with many poets who remain very loyal to us, as we are to them. We don't consciously continue to build our brand, but are content to maintain a presence just as it is now.

What parts of the publishing process do you do in-house and which do you outsource?

Outsource – Distribution and printing. In-house – everything else except the very occasional cover.

Any funny publishing stories?

Typo time! Emails:
In 2011, I was delighted that Carol Ann Duffy had sent an original poem for our anthology Soul Feathers (to aid Macmillan Cancer Support). I sent a block email to encourage

others to submit and in my excitement referred to her as *'the Poppet Laureate.'* How many levels is that wrong on....?
And last year an Indigo poet emailed me with details of readings she'd arranged, seven over two weeks. I meant to say how I love busy poets – but it was sent as *"...I really love a busty poet."* I only realised it when she replied *"Sorry Ronnie, I can't help you on that one, but I'll keep on arranging readings if you like!"*

You can perhaps see why Dawn handles the proofing, but a while back she spotted her typo in one of her magazines before it went to print. The Xmas issue had a poem containing *"..and the children singing ghostly carols"*. She had typed *"..and the children singing ghastly carols"*
That's all folks!

Resources

Review Platform List – online and print magazines

- Sabotage Reviews (accepts prewritten reviews or review requests)
- London Grip (accepts prewritten reviews or review requests)
- The Blue Nib (accepts prewritten reviews or review requests)
- Neon Literary Magazine (accepts prewritten reviews or review requests)
- Kissing Dynamite (accepts prewritten)
- Royal Rose (accepts prewritten)
- Riggwelter (accepts prewritten)
- Mad Hatter Reviews (accepts review requests)

National Newspapers

- The Guardian review@theguardian.com
- The Times books@thetimes.co.uk
- The Spectator editor@spectator.co.uk
- The Telegraph DTnews@telegraph.co.uk/stnews@telegraph.co.uk

Printers "UK"

- Iprint Global
- Biddles
- 4Edge LTD
- Swallowtail (FSC certified)
- TJ International
- Ingram Spark/lightning source (Print on demand)
- Clays Ltd

Blog Tour Operators

Fly on the Wall Blog Tours (poetry specialism)

Isabelle Kenyon

https://www.flyonthewallpoetry.co.uk/author-services

isabellekenyon@hotmail.co.uk

Random Things Tours

Anne Cater

https://randomthingsthroughmyletterbox.blogspot.com/p/services-to-publishers-authors-blog.html

anne.lcdp@hotmail.co.uk

Book On The Bright Side

Sarah Hardy

https://bytheletterbookreviews.com/botbspublicity-promo-services/

sarah.botbspublicity@gmail.com

Historical Fiction Virtual Book Tours

Amy Bruno

http://hfvirtualbooktours.com/tour-packages/

hfvirtualbooktours@gmail.com

Rachel's Random Resources

Rachel Gilbey

https://www.rachelsrandomresources.com/for-authors

rachel@rachelsrandomresources.com

Damppebbles Blog Tours

(crime/thriller fiction only)

Emma Welton

https://damppebbles.com/damppebbles-blog-tours/

damppebbles@gmail.com

WOW! Women on Writing Blog Tours

Nicole Pyles

https://wow-womenonwriting.com/contact.php

nicole@wow-womenonwriting.com

About Fly on the Wall Press

A publisher with a conscience.
Publishing high quality anthologies on pressing issues, chapbooks and poetry products, from exceptional poets around the globe.
Founded in 2018 by founding editor, Isabelle Kenyon.

Other publications:

Please Hear What I'm Not Saying
(February 2018. Anthology, profits to Mind.)
Persona Non Grata
(October 2018. Anthology, profits to Shelter and Crisis Aid UK.)
Bad Mommy/Stay Mommy by Elisabeth Horan
(May 2019. Chapbook.)
The Woman With An Owl Tattoo by Anne Walsh Donnelly
(May 2019. Chapbook.)
the sea refuses no river by Bethany Rivers
(June 2019. Chapbook.)
White Light White Peak by Simon Corble
(July 2019. Artist's Book.)
Second Life by Karl Tearney
(July 2019. Full collection)
The Dogs of Humanity by Colin Dardis
(August 2019. Chapbook.)

Social Media:

@fly_press (Twitter)
@flyonthewall_poetry (Instagram)
@flyonthewallpoetry (Facebook)
www.flyonthewallpoetry.co.uk